MELCHIZEDEK
A SHADOW OF CHRIST

by Jerry Scheumann

Publishing
Angel
Climbing

Melchizedek: A Shadow of Christ
Written by Jerry Scheumann

Transcribed and edited by Lisa Soland
Text copyright © 2023 Jerry Scheumann

Published in 2023 by:
Climbing Angel Publishing
PO Box 32381
Knoxville, Tennessee 37930
http://www.ClimbingAngel.com

First Edition: August 2023
Printed in the United States of America

Cover painting: By Marie-Lan Nguyen/Jastrow: 'Melchizedek and Abraham', attributed to Colin Nouailher (between 1560 & 1570) held by the Louvre.

Graphic Design: Climbing Angel Publishing

ISBN: 978-1-956218-29-9
Library of Congress Control Number: 2023911605

This book is dedicated to
Ashlee

"You are the one 'whom my soul loves.'"
(Song of Solomon 1:7)

4

The Single Sermon Series

INTRODUCTION

In Hebrews 7, the author is writing to believing ethnic Jews who were tempted to turn away from Christ and return to the Old Covenant. They wanted to go back to the Levitical priesthood, to the sacrifices of bulls and goats offered up for sin. The book of Hebrews warns, *"If you do that, if you forsake Christ, and go back to the shadows of the Old Covenant, there is no hope for salvation. There is no sacrifice for sin if you reject Christ."* To compel them to press on to faith in Christ, the author spends chapter after chapter in the middle of Hebrews, showing the superiority of the priesthood of Jesus Christ compared to the Old Testament Levitical priesthood.

The subject of Christ being our High Priest might not strike some as important today, but having a qualified high priest is essential to save us and forgive us of our sins. In the Old Testament, the priest ministered on behalf of the people of God on account of their sins. The people of God could not present a sacrifice; only the priest was qualified by God to do so. And all of this protocol represented a shadow of the greater priest to come—our Lord Jesus Christ.

The office of a high priest teaches us that we, as sinners, cannot approach a holy God in our sin. We can't come just as we are without a priest because "God is a consuming fire" (Heb. 12:29 NIV). God's "eyes are too pure to look on evil" (Hab. 1:13). " For all have sinned and fall short of the glory of God" (Rom. 3:23). We cannot approach God and have fellowship with Him. We need one uniquely qualified who ministers on our behalf and offers up a sacrifice for sins so that we can be forgiven and be reconciled to God.

From Chapter 4:14 through Chapter 10:18, the author of Hebrews expounds on the significance of how Jesus is the Great High Priest after the order of Melchizedek. He devotes more than five chapters on this theme. But after only just introducing the theme and writing about its significance for about a chapter, he interrupts his flow of thought and addresses the Hebrew Christians: "About this we have much to say, and it is hard to explain, since you have become dull of hearing" (Heb. 5:11). In other words, *"We have much to say about Christ being the High Priest after the order of Melchizedek, and it's hard to explain since you have become dull of hearing."* The Jewish believers had become spiritually lazy and hard of hearing. They no longer wanted to hear about how Christ is the Great High Priest after the order of Melchizedek. So the author admonishes them and says, *"You need to move on from spiritual infancy. You need to move on from these elemental principles of the faith. You need to move on to more fundamental, deeper truths about who Christ is, including Him being our Great High Priest."* At the end of Hebrews 6, the author provides an assurance of salvation rooted in God's faithful promises and Christ's finished work, and then he resumes his teaching on Melchizedek and says:

> *...where Jesus has gone as a forerunner on our behalf, having become a high priest forever after the order of Melchizedek.*
> (Hebrews 6:20)

Do you see what the author is doing? He admonishes them for their sluggishness of heart, saying, *"You don't have a desire to hear about these things. You need to move on. You need to have a greater desire for the Word of God,"* etc. Then he picks right up where he left off and teaches them about Melchizedek and how he points us forward to Christ.

These verses in Hebrews teach us a fundamental principle: it is the Word of God, not man's preferences, that must dictate what is preached week by week. It must not be the preferences of the preacher or the congregation. It is imperative that we be led by the Word of God.

If you asked the Hebrew Christians of the day, *"Do you have the desire to learn about how Christ is the Great High Priest after the order of Melchizedek?"* they would say, *"I don't see how that could possibly be important to my life."* But God knew that they needed to hear this, so by His Spirit, He inspired the author to keep preaching on this topic for another four chapters.

For decades now there has been present in many churches in America what is called the "seeker-sensitive movement." This movement requires that the entire worship service be changed, morphed, and adjusted to suit the preferences of man, particularly unbelievers. The sermon suffers the most. Difficult doctrine is shunned and, in most cases, avoided altogether. Any possibly offensive topics are left to the side, and the sermon becomes a sort of self-help pep talk. *"Here's how you can live a more fulfilled life,"* rather than declaring, *"Here is what Jesus Christ has done, and here is how you can have eternal life in Him."*

The great error in the "seeker-sensitive movement" is that it doesn't consider who the *true seeker* is. There is a true seeker, but it is not man. The true seeker who we must keep in mind when we're worshiping is God. Read what Jesus says in John 4:23:

> *But the hour is coming, and is now here, when the true worshipers will worship the Father in spirit and truth, for the Father is seeking such people to worship him.*

The intent of true worship must be to please the Ultimate Seeker, God Himself. We should desire to offer worship in spirit and truth that is pleasing and glorifying to Him.

Of course, the church ought to be friendly, welcome outsiders, and let them know we are happy they are worshiping with us. Yes, we want to explain the Word of God and make it understandable, but our focus in all that we do must be to glorify God. We should want *Him* to be pleased and honored. God has ordained that we need to be taught not just part of the Bible but the whole council of God.

> *Therefore I testify to you this day that I am innocent of the blood of all, for I did not shrink from declaring to you the whole counsel of God.*
> (Acts 20:26-27)

Pastors have an obligation from God to preach the entire council of God—Genesis to Revelation—including parts that we may not have a great desire to learn.

Perhaps you may not see the immediate relevance of Melchizedek to your life. You may not see his priesthood as essential or relevant to your faith, but we need to have enough faith to trust that God knows better than we do. So, when we come to the Word of God, we must say, *"All of Your gospel is breathed out by You, oh God, and it is useful, including all about Melchizedek."* It is central to our salvation and profitable for our edification, or God would not have placed it in the Bible.

WHO IS MELCHIZEDEK?

We learn about Melchizedek in only four verses of the Old Testament—three verses from Genesis 14 and one from Psalm 110:

And Melchizedek king of Salem brought out bread and wine. (He was priest of God Most High.) And he blessed him and said, "Blessed be Abram by God Most High, Possessor of heaven and earth; and blessed be God Most High, who has delivered your enemies into your hand!" And Abram gave him a tenth of everything.
(Genesis 14:18-20)

The Lord has sworn and will not change his mind, "You are a priest forever after the order of Melchizedek."
(Psalms 110:4)

Hebrews 7:1-2 are the only New Testament verses that provide us with additional information about this mysterious man.

> *For this Melchizedek, king of Salem, priest of the Most High God, met Abraham returning from the slaughter of the kings and blessed him, and to him Abraham apportioned a tenth part of everything. He is first, by translation of his name, king of righteousness, and then he is also king of Salem, that is, king of peace.*
> (Hebrews 7:1-2)

The story of Melchizedek begins with a coalition of four evil kings waging war against five other kings in the region of Sodom and Gomorrah. The four kings routed these five other kings, captured many people, and took off with their possessions. One of those captured was Lot, the nephew of Abraham. When Abraham heard of the defeat of those in Sodom and Gomorrah and the capture of his nephew, he rallied over 300 of his trained men, pursued the four evil kings, engaged them in battle, and God gave Abraham and his men a mighty victory. They rescued those held captive, along with Lot, and returned with the stolen possessions.

As they were returning from the fight, this mysterious Melchizedek appears. He meets Abraham, and we read that two primary things occurred—Abraham gives Melchizedek a tenth, or a tithe, of all the spoils he collected from the military conquest. Then Melchizedek blesses Abraham. These two actions demonstrate Melchizedek's superiority, a superiority even over the blessed Abraham, the patriarch of the faith. Additionally, Melchizedek's dual identity as king of Salem and priest of the Most High God further establish that this is a great man indeed.

Who is this man? Some have suggested that Melchizedek is a pre-incarnate form of Jesus Christ. Jesus does reveal Himself in different Christophanies in the Old Testament. The word Christophany combines two Greek words—Christos, which means "Christ," and phainein, which means "to appear." So, a Christophany is a pre-incarnate appearance of Christ.

For example, we see a Christophany in Joshua 5 when the commander of the army of the Lord appeared to Joshua before his conquest of the Promised Land and called for Joshua to remove his sandals because he was on holy ground.

When Joshua was by Jericho, he lifted up his eyes and looked, and behold, a man was standing before him with his drawn sword in his hand. And Joshua went to him and said to him, "Are you for us, or for our adversaries?" And he said, "No; but I am the commander of the army of the Lord. Now I have come." And

Joshua fell on his face to the earth and worshiped and said to him, "What does my lord say to his servant?" And the commander of the Lord's army said to Joshua, "Take off your sandals from your feet, for the place where you are standing is holy." And Joshua did so.
(Joshua 5:13-15)

We see another Christophany in Christ's appearance to Jacob in Genesis 32:24-31:

And Jacob was left alone. And a man wrestled with him until the breaking of the day. When the man saw that he did not prevail against Jacob, he touched his hip socket, and Jacob's hip was put out of joint as he wrestled with him. Then he said, "Let me go, for the day has broken." But Jacob said, "I will not let you go unless you bless me." And he said to him, "What is your name?" And he said, "Jacob." Then he said, "Your name shall no longer be called Jacob, but Israel, for you have striven with God and with men, and have prevailed." Then Jacob asked him, "Please tell me your name." But he said, "Why is it that you ask my name?" And there he blessed him. So Jacob called the name of the place Peniel, saying, "For I have seen God face to face, and yet my life has been delivered." The sun rose upon him as he passed Penuel, limping because of his hip.

The man wrestled with Jacob all night long. Jacob recognizes the man's superiority and says, "I will not let you go unless you bless me" (Gen. 32:26). Then, at daybreak, this man touches Jacob's hip socket to put it out of place and says, "Your name shall no longer be called Jacob, but Israel, for you have striven with God and with men, and have prevailed." Jacob responds by saying that he has seen the face of God. Both of these examples are clearly pre-incarnate forms or appearances of Jesus Christ.

There are some people who point to Hebrews 7:3 to argue that Melchizedek is a pre-incarnate form of Christ.

He is without father or mother or genealogy, having neither beginning of days nor end of life, but resembling the Son of God he continues a priest forever.
(Hebrews 7:3)

Some interpret the description of Melchizedek as being "without father or mother or genealogy" to be referring to the eternal second person of the Trinity. But there is good reason from this verse that we shouldn't interpret Melchizedek literally as Christ but as a real man, a Canaanite king, who was a type or shadow of Christ.

There is a park near where I live in Vermont called Plymouth State Park. All throughout the grounds are 80-foot-high majestic Eastern White Pines. If you were at the park and saw the shadows cast by the pine trees, you would not marvel at the shadows. The reality of the Eastern White Pine is not found in its shadows but in the soaring heights of the tree itself. And so Melchizedek, as a *type* of Christ, points forward to the greater reality found in our Savior, Jesus.

The consistent interpretation of the church throughout the millennia is that Melchizedek was not literally Christ, but a type of Christ. We see a clue in verse 3 that points us in that direction.

> *He is without father or mother or genealogy, having neither beginning of days nor end of life, but **resembling the Son of God** he continues a priest forever.*
> (Hebrews 7:3)

Scripture does not say he "is the Son of God," but that he *resembles* the Son of God. Melchizedek was not a Christophany. He was not a preincarnate form of the Son of God. He resembles the Son of God and functions as a type or shadow of Christ.

Throughout Hebrews, we see that Jesus Christ is foreshadowed in the Old Covenant by these types or shadows that point forward to Christ. In Hebrews 3:5-6, we read that Moses was faithful in God's house as a servant; he too was a shadow of Jesus Christ who is faithful in all of God's houses but as a son.

Now Moses was faithful in all God's house as a servant, to testify to the things that were to be spoken later, but Christ is faithful over God's house as a son. And we are his house, if indeed we hold fast our confidence and our boasting in our hope.
(Hebrews 3:5-6)

And Joshua, too, is a shadow of Jesus. Joshua led the people of God into victory over their enemies, the Canaanites, and gave them rest. But Jesus is the greater Joshua who defeated the far greater enemies of sin, Satan, and death, and thus secures a heavenly rest for the people of God for all eternity.

When the sun sets in the town where we live, Ludlow, Vermont, it sets behind the Okemo Mountain range. And at the end of the day, the mountain casts a very long shadow over the town. One would not look at that shadow and think it appears out of nowhere every single day. The long shadow over Ludlow each evening points to the far more majestic 3,000-foot-high mountain behind the town.

Melchizedek resembles the Son of God. He is a shadow of the Son of God. The greatness of Melchizedek, which is emphasized in this passage, points forward to the far greater greatness of Jesus Christ.

FIVE WAYS MELCHIZEDEK IS SUPERIOR TO THE LEVITICAL PRIESTHOOD

In this passage of Hebrews, there are five ways in which we see the superiority of the Melchizedek priesthood compared to the Levitical priesthood of the Old Testament, and how that points forward to the far surpassing greatness of Jesus Christ and the salvation we have in Him.

1. Melchizedek was a King of Righteousness

The author begins his exegesis of the significance of Melchizedek in Hebrews 7:2.

He is first, by translation of his name,
king of righteousness...

Melchizedek's name consists of two parts. The first is 'Melchi' from the Hebrew word 'Melek,' which means 'king,' and then 'zedek,' which means 'righteousness.' The name Melchizedek means 'king of righteousness.' What's striking is that he is not only a king but also a priest. Holding both offices makes him far superior to the Levitical priesthood.

...priest of the Most High God...
(Hebrews 7:1)

Under the Old Covenant, God ordained that the line of the priests and kings be separate. The kings were descended from the line of David, from the tribe of Judah. And the priests were descended from Aaron, from the tribe of Levi—hence, *Levitical* priests. God ordained that kings could not function as priests. In 2 Chronicles 26:16-21, when King Uzziah sought to act as a priest and burn incense on the altar, he was opposed by 80 priests of the Lord who said:

...and they withstood King Uzziah and said to him, "It is not for you, Uzziah, to burn incense to the Lord, but for the priests, the sons of Aaron, who are consecrated to burn incense. Go out of the sanctuary, for you have done wrong, and it will bring you no honor from the Lord God."
(2 Chronicles 26:18)

King Uzziah was proud and was not satisfied with his office of king. He wanted to function as a priest as well. In response to the priests' rebuke, King Uzziah became very angry, defiantly proceeded to burn incense, and immediately leprosy broke out on his forehead. Leprosy was a skin disease, and according to the Old Testament ceremonial law, it made one unclean. The priests saw the leprosy and immediately called out to King Uzziah and got him out of the temple. Because of his arrogance in wanting to function as king *and* priest, King Uzziah spent the rest of his days unclean and was unable to re-enter the temple.

A king could not function as a priest, and a priest could not be a king. But here is Melchizedek, who is ruling and reigning as king and also ministering on behalf of sinners as a priest. And in the land of ancient Canaan, where all the kings were wicked, we encounter Melchizedek, a king of righteousness. This points forward to Christ, who is both a priest and a king, and whose reign as king is one of perfect righteousness.

We read in Hebrews 1:9 that it was because of Christ's perfect righteousness that he has been exalted as King:

> *You have loved righteousness and*
> *hated wickedness;* therefore God, your
> God, has anointed you with the oil of gladness
> beyond your companions.
> (Hebrews 1:9)

Upon Jesus' resurrection and ascension, He was exalted as King of kings and Lord of lords because He loved righteousness and hated wickedness. His kingdom is established in perfect righteousness. Everything that Jesus decrees, judges, and does is according to the righteous law of God. And not only is Jesus the King who acts righteously in all He does, but as the righteous king, He also ensures by His mighty power that His people will be righteous as well.

Daniel 9 speaks of the Christ to come as one who brings in an everlasting righteousness.

*Seventy weeks are decreed about your people and your holy city, to finish the transgression, to put an end to sin, and to atone for iniquity, **to bring in everlasting righteousness**, to seal both vision and prophet, and to anoint a most holy place.*
(Daniel 9:24)

Christ accomplished this by laying down His life on the cross outside of Jerusalem. There He suffered greatly, not on account of His own sin, for He had none. He was completely righteous. But He suffered as a sacrifice for our sins, bearing the punishment and penalty that was due us for our transgressions and unrighteousness. He did this so that by faith in His name, we might be forgiven of all of our sins. And because of His act, all our sin has been placed upon Him on the cross. And His perfect righteousness has been credited to us, clothing us as a spotless garment.

Jesus has also given us His Spirit to empower us to walk in righteousness in our thoughts, desires, and actions. Whereas apart from God's grace, we were dead in our trespasses and sins (Eph. 2:1) and in bondage to all manner of sinful desires. But now, by the work of the Holy Spirit, we have been born again, and by His great power, we can live a life that is pleasing to the Lord. As we walk by the Spirit of God in obedience to His commands, we will grow in holiness and righteousness.

His reign is not only established in righteousness, but His grace makes wretchedly sinful people like you and me righteous through His work. What an awesome king Jesus is!

2. Melchizedek was a King of Peace

He is first, by translation of his name, king of righteousness, and then he is also king of Salem, that is, king of peace.
(Hebrews 7:2)

Salem was later called Jerusalem, the city of David, where God's king rules. But what is emphasized here is that the word Salem means "peace." So, Melchizedek is a king of peace, making him far greater than the Levitical priests. And again, all this points forward to Jesus Christ, who is the King of Peace.

> *For to us a child is born, to us a son is given;*
> *and the government shall be upon his shoulder,*
> *and his name shall be called*
> *Wonderful Counselor, Mighty God,*
> *Everlasting Father, **Prince of Peace**.*
> (Isaiah 9:6)

Jesus, the Prince of Peace has come to make peace with mankind. He does so with us who were once in rebellion against Him. And how does Jesus establish this peace? He does so through His work of righteousness here on earth. The fact that Jesus is the King of righteousness and the King of peace goes together because, in our sin, we don't have peace with God. We don't have communion with God. Scripture says that we were enemies of God (Rom. 5:8). We were opposed to Him, and He was opposed to us because of our sin. But because Jesus shed his precious blood for sinners and credits His righteous life to us, received by faith, we now have peace with God.

God's Word in Romans 5:1 says this:

> *Therefore, since we have been justified by*
> *faith, we have peace with God through our*
> *Lord Jesus Christ.*

To be "justified" means that we are declared righteous, and righteous not by our own goodness, not by our own works, but by the work of our Great High Priest. We are justified by Jesus' atoning work for sin and by His righteous life credited to us. We receive this as a gift by faith, and God looks upon us and declares, "Not guilty! Righteous!"

The two offices of Christ (priest and king) and the two aspects of His kingship (King of righteousness and King of peace) go together. It is because He is the King of righteousness *and* the King of peace that we have peace with God through Jesus Christ.

3. Melchizedek is a Kind of Forever Priest

He is without father or mother or genealogy,
having neither beginning of days nor end of life,
but resembling the Son of God he
continues a priest forever.
(Hebrews 7:3)

If Melchizedek was a real Canaanite king, how can it be said that he is without "beginning of days" and without "end of life?" If he was a man like us, how can this be true?

Throughout Genesis, everyone who is anyone has a genealogy. We are given the genealogies of Adam, Noah, and Abraham. We read who their parents were, how old they were, when they had their first child, and how old they were when they died. But even though Melchizedek is so much greater than Abraham, we read nothing about his mother or father, or when he was born, how long he lived, and when he died. So, according to what's written, or rather, what's *not* written, it is as if Melchizedek is without mother or father or genealogy. This makes his priesthood far superior to the Levitical priesthood.

For the Levitical priests, everything hinged upon who their parents were. They had to be from the tribe of Levi. They had to be a descendant of Aaron. They could serve and were qualified to serve because of their legal descent regarding who their ancestors were. What does this mean when we see that nothing is said about Melchizedek's ancestors? His qualification to serve as high priest is not on account of his ancestral lineage because nothing is said about his genealogy. Rather, he is qualified to serve as priest because he has a kind of eternal priesthood. We read nothing of his death, and it is as if eternity is ascribed to him. This is what qualified Melchizedek to serve.

King David meditates on this truth regarding Melchizedek and says this regarding the Messiah to come in Psalm 110:

The Lord has sworn and will not change his
mind, "You are a priest forever after
the order of Melchizedek."
(Psalm 110:4)

Melchizedek had a type of forever priesthood, and David says that the Christ to come will be a priest in his line, a priest who serves forever. Again, all of this points forward to the greatness of Christ, who is qualified to serve as our priest, not because of who He descended from but because He has an *eternal priesthood*. He is the one who is truly without "beginning of days." The Son of God has always existed. He is the one who is truly without "end of life."

In the beginning was the Word, and the Word
was with God, and the Word was God.
He was in the beginning with God.
(John 1:1-2)

Jesus died on the cross, was placed in the tomb, and then what happened on the third day? He overcame death. He defeated death. He rose again from the dead. And Jesus is alive forevermore. Amen!

When I saw him, I fell at his feet as though
dead. But he laid his right hand on
me, saying, "Fear not, I am the first and
the last, and the living one. I died, and

behold I am alive forevermore, *and I have
the keys of Death and Hades."*
(Revelation 1:17-18)

Christ's eternal priesthood is far superior
to the Levitical priesthood. The Old Testament
priests could not continue in ministry because
death prevented them. They would minister
for a few decades, perhaps, and then they
would die, and their ministry would come to
an end. But Christ has a high priesthood
because of his indestructible life. He has
a *forever priesthood.* He doesn't just minister
for decades or centuries. He ministers for all
eternity.

*In the one case tithes are received by mortal
men, but in the other case, by one of whom
it is testified that he lives.*
(Hebrews 7:8)

Levitical priests would receive tithes from
their Israelite brothers, but these priests
would die because they were mortal. But in the
other case, Abraham gave tithes to Melchizedek, and it is testified of Melchizedek that
he lives. He is not presented as a mortal man.
So, what makes the Melchizedekian
priesthood so great? It is a forever priesthood
foreshadowed by Melchizedek and fulfilled in
the person of Jesus Christ.

4. Melchizedek Received a Tithe from Abraham

The fourth way that Melchizedek's priesthood is greater is because he received a tithe from Abraham.

> *See how great this man was to whom Abraham the patriarch gave a tenth of the spoils! And those descendants of Levi who receive the priestly office have a commandment in the law to take tithes from the people, that is, from their brothers, though these also are descended from Abraham.*
> (Hebrews 7:4-5)

God commanded in the Old Testament law that the people of God were to give a tenth, or a *tithe*, to those who labored in the ministry of the Lord—to the descendants of Levi serving as priests. These tithes demonstrated one's honored status as ministering on God's behalf. So, the Israelites gave a tithe to the priests.

> *But this man* [Melchizedek] *who does not have his descent from them received tithes from Abraham and blessed him who had the promises. It is beyond dispute that the inferior is blessed by the superior.*
> (Hebrews 7:6-7)

Melchizedek does not descend from Abraham. He doesn't descend from Levi, the great-grandson of Abraham. He doesn't have his descent from any of them at all, yet he's receiving tithes from Abraham, the father, and patriarch of the faith, the great-grandfather of Levi from whom the priestly line derives. This demonstrates that Melchizedek is a far greater priest than the Levitical priests. He's receiving tithes from Abraham, the ancestor of Levi.

One might even say that Levi himself, who receives tithes, paid tithes through Abraham, for he was still in the loins of his ancestor when Melchizedek met him.
(Hebrews 7:9-10)

So who is greater? The line of Levi or Melchizedek? The answer is Melchizedek. Abraham gives a tenth of all the spoils to Melchizedek because of Melchizedek's privileged status as a priest of God. The author of Hebrews is further establishing the superiority of the Melchizedekian priesthood. To go back to the Old Covenant and the Levitical priesthood is to go back to that which is inferior. It is to go back to the shadows. Here you have Melchizedek, who received a tenth from Abraham, the father of the faith. And all of this directs us forward to Jesus the Priest after the order of Melchizedek. It shows the far greater worthiness of Jesus Christ.

And now, we see the final reason why Christ's priesthood in the order of Melchizedek is far superior to the Levitical priesthood of the Old Testament.

5. Melchizedek Blessed Abraham

*But this man who does not have his descent from them received tithes from Abraham **and blessed him who had the promises.***
(Hebrews 7:6)

Abraham was no unimportant man. He was great. He had received the promises of God. God had called him out, promising that He would lavish His blessings upon him, and that His plan of salvation would come through his descendants. And though we see that Abraham had the promises, we see that Melchizedek blessed Abraham.

This sort of blessing is not the kind of praying we might do for one another. *"God, I pray that you bless Jim. I pray that you bless Betty."* Melchizedek's blessing symbolized one being in a position of greater authority, pronouncing God's covenant blessings to be upon another individual.

In the book of Genesis, Isaac blessed Jacob rather than Esau and pronounced God's blessing upon him. Jacob blessed his grandsons Ephraim and Manasseh. And so with Abraham, we have one who is so great and possesses the promises, and yet Melchizedek blesses him.

> *It is beyond dispute that the inferior*
> *is blessed by the superior.*
> (Hebrews 7:7)

In other words, the one who is "blessing" is greater than the one who is being "blessed." This shows us how much greater Melchizedek is than one so highly exalted as Abraham. Melchizedek is the superior one, for he is blessing Abraham, the inferior one.

Again, what does this say about the Levitical priests who descend from Abraham? It reveals that Melchizedek's priesthood is far greater than theirs. All this points forward to Christ, who is our Great High Priest. It's in Christ that we receive God's blessings, and we welcome God's blessings only in and through Christ. Outside of Christ, God's Word says we are under a curse on account of our sin because of our failure to obey the law of God. But Jesus has redeemed us from the curse of the law so that in Him, the blessing of Abraham might come to us.

SEE HOW GREAT CHRIST IS!

Jesus' priesthood is not simply a continuation of the Old Covenant priesthood. No, it is far superior! Jesus' ministry does not continue the status quo of the Levitical priests. His ministry to sinners is far greater and more effectual to save sinners in their great need. You don't need to worry about whether this priest is powerful enough, for He is the *King of Righteousness* and the *King of Peace*. You don't have to worry about Jesus' ministry coming to an end and there being no hope of salvation because Jesus is a *Forever Priest*. You don't have to worry about whether He's worthy to serve because Abraham and, in a sense, Levi paid tithe or tribute to the priests of this order. And you don't have to worry about His greatness and favor, for He is the *Superior One* who blesses all who come to Him.

The devil loves to crush and destroy us on account of our sin. He will accuse us to God, saying, *"Look what they've done! Look at the way they've broken the law of God! There's no hope of salvation because they've disobeyed You!"* This approach is so nefarious because there is some truth in what Satan is saying. There is indeed no hope in ourselves because of our sin, so we must look *outside* ourselves. We must look to our Great High Priest, who ministers on our behalf. Look at His qualifications. Look at His perfections. Look at His love. Look at His mercy. Look at His finished work. Look at His blessing and favor.

The good news of Jesus being our High Priest is this—your sin doesn't have to be the final word because we have a Great High Priest. Isn't that good news?! No matter how wretchedly you have sinned and rebelled against God, your sin does not have to have the final word because Jesus is the Great High Priest, and His ministry is not for the righteous. His ministry is for sinners. Jesus is a High Priest ministering on behalf of sinners. We need not look at our sin and say, *"There's no way I can be reconciled to God. There's no way I can be forgiven. There's no hope for the future. I know what I've done."*

Look to your Great High Priest who ministers on behalf of sinners. If we come to Christ in humble faith, turning from our sins and trusting in His work of salvation on our behalf, we will be forgiven, we will be made righteous, we will be washed, and we will be reconciled to God. This is the salvation that we have in our Lord and Savior, Jesus Christ, our Great Eternal High Priest.

PRAYER

Father, thank you for how you give your Spirit to us to provide us with an understanding of Your wonderful salvation. You inspired men of old—the prophets and your apostles—to write precisely what you intended them to write. We pray that we would come to see how you have ordained salvation through this "type and shadow" we discover through Melchizedek. These verses about Melchizedek help us understand what the ministry of Christ is like as our Great High Priest. So, Father, I pray that you bring understanding, clarity, and a greater appreciation of our mighty Savior, Jesus Christ. Remind us that He is forever ministering on our behalf and has paid the full and complete price so we can be reconciled to God. Assure us of Your great love for sinners like us. We bless you, Lord, and praise you in Jesus' name. Amen.

ABOUT CLIMBING ANGEL
PUBLISHING

Climbing Angel Publishing exists for the purpose of sharing stories of hope and encouragement, aiding in the gathering together of community, and supporting the process of betterment. The following books are available at ClimbingAngel.com and major bookstores.

ADULT BOOKS: (Romans 8:28-30)

In His Image by Sam Polson
(English, Romanian, & Mandarin)
By Faith by Sam Polson (English & Romanian)
My Birthday Gift to Jesus by Lisa Soland
Without Ceasing by Dr. Dennis Davidson
SonLight: Daily Light from the Pages of God's Word
by Sam Polson
Corona Victus: Conquering the Virus of Fear
by Sam Polson (English & Romanian)
Art Bushing: His Diary, Letters, & Photographs of WWII
by Art Bushing
*Art & Dotty: His Diary, Their Letters & Photographs of
WWII* by Art Bushing
Trimisul by Stan Johnson (Romanian)
Life Changing Prayer by Sam Polson
The Climbing Angel Christmas Treasury, variety of authors
J. Calvin Coolidge: Letters from the Korean War
by J. Calvin Coolidge
Stories from Kingman, AZ: The Heart of Historic Route 66
by Loren B. Wilson
*Pathways: Ancient Paths from the Pages of the Old
Testament* by Sam Polson

THE SINGLE SERMON SERIES: (1 Peter 3:15)

Jesus is Alive! by Mike Sager
My Mother's Bible by Sam Polson
The Lost Boys by Jake Bishop
Melchizedek: A Shadow of Christ by Jerry Scheumann

CHILDREN'S BOOKS: (Philippians 4:8)

The Christmas Tree Angel by Lisa Soland
The Unmade Moose by Lisa Soland
Thump by Lisa Soland
Somebunny To Love by Lisa Soland
(English & Mandarin)
The Truth About God's Rainbow by Lisa Soland
God's Promises by Lisa Soland
The Boy & The Bagel Necklace by Lisa Soland
God's Hands and Feet by Lisa Soland
I Like To Be Quiet by Joni Caldwell
Wheels Off! by Karlie Saumier
Ella's Trip of a Lifetime by Melanie Ewbank
Because You Are Mine by Gayle Childress Greene
Jeremy Plays the Blues by Amy Oden Simpson
Bad Hair Day by Jasmyne Simpkins
I Like To Read by Joni Caldwell
Trunks Up! by Karlie Saumier
Perusha's Paradise by Bette Reed Smith
Ruby and the Treasure Within by Tonya Celeste Hobbs
Abby, the Wonder Dog & her Warrior Princess
by Melanie Ewbank
The Christmas Coat by Lisa Soland
Danger Around the Bend by Karlie Saumier

www.ingramcontent.com/pod-product-compliance
Lightning Source LLC
Chambersburg PA
CBHW070957120626
46546CB00004B/1656